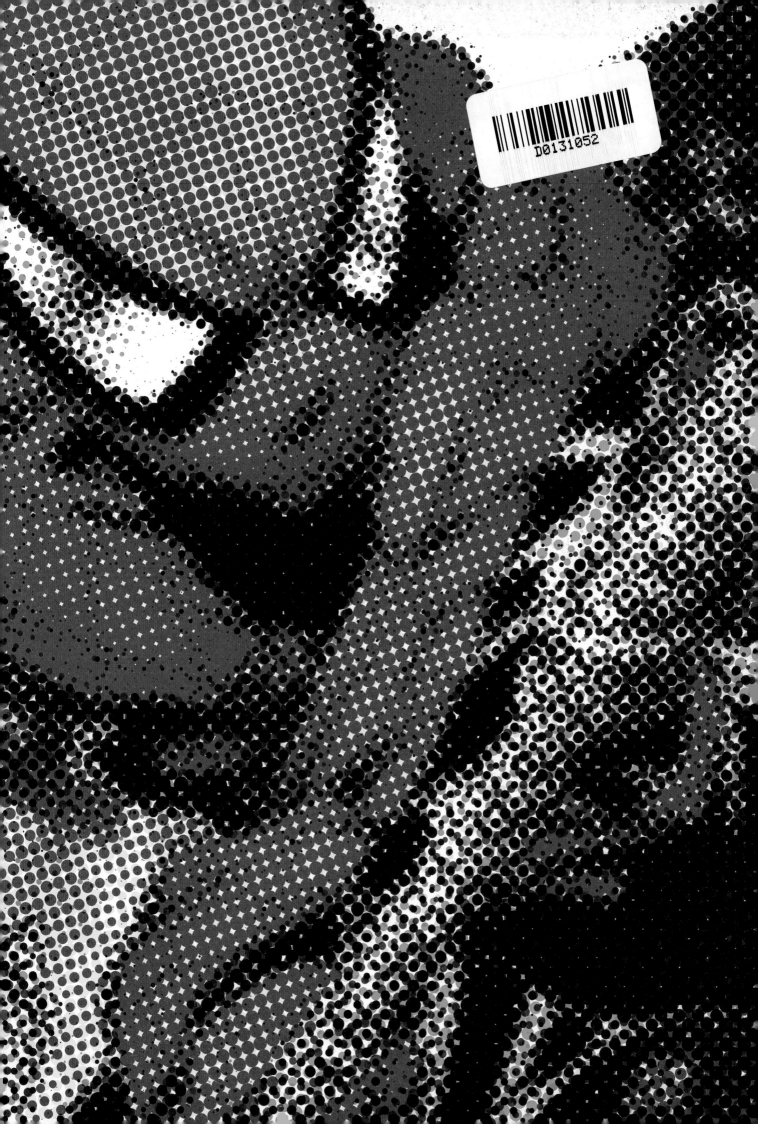

COMIC HEROES

6
THE TOP 25 HEROES

The top 25 best superheroes revealed in our massive feature!

BORN TO BE BAD

Where would our heroes be without villains? We take a look at 20 of comics' meanest menaces...

30

36 STAR WARS COMICS!

Loved The Force Awakens and want more? Try these comics!

X-MEN 52

Everything you need to know about your favourite mutant superheroes!

INSIDE

SPIDEY QUIZ!

Test your Spidey-sense with our Super Spider-Man Quiz!

60

THE TOP 25 HEROES

Over the next few pages, you'll discover the top 25 superheroes! From obscure characters to your biggest favourites, there's bound to be something for everyone in this list!

25 SILVER SURFER

When we first caught sight of Norrin Radd in *Fantastic Four* #48, he was little more than a jumped up messenger, a Herald of Galactus just doing his job. But the Silver Surfer quickly became one of the most recognisable and cool creations, an instantly iconic slice of cosmic Marvel who went on to have a career that has spanned more than 40 years so far.

Stan Lee has always been a big fan of the Surfer. "I got more philosophy into the Silver Surfer than anything I ever wrote," he said. "He was always giving his opinions about life, liberty and the pursuit of happiness. I liked him because he was so offbeat. I think those 17 issues of *Silver Surfer* that I wrote and that John Buscema

drew are the best 17 comics that have ever been done."

A wonderfully complicated, character who had travelled across the universe, the Silver Surfer was a million miles away from the shiny, smiley faces of the Fantastic Four or the wise-cracking Spider-Man. He's an intergalactic traveller with sadness behind his eyes, a heartbreaking backstory and with more humanity than most, well, humans.

The last word here must go to Jack Kirby, the man who first dreamed him up "The Silver Surfer is a fallen angel, and when Galactus relegated him to Earth he stayed on Earth. They were figures that had never before been used in comics, and of course they were the first gods."

FIRST APPEARANCE FANTASTIC FOUR #48 CURRENT STATUS ALIVE

24 PUNISHER

After the killing of his wife and children at the hands of the New York mob, Frank Castle became the Punisher: a disturbingly dark vigilante who, controversially, had no time for triflings such as mercy. He is just as much of a monster as those he fought.

Created by writer Gerry Conway and artists John Romita Sr and Ross Andru, he made his first appearance in 1974's *Amazing Spider-Man* #129 as a vigilante who had tasked himself with hunting down Spider-Man for a murder he didn't commit.

He was introduced as a master shooter and an expert strategist – appearing to have no qualms about killing gangsters, but a

major problem with killing Spider-Man dishonourably. The character became not only a hit – going on to appear on a regular basis alongside Captain America and Nightcrawler in the '70s and '80s – but one of Marvel's most interesting characters. Is it really one tragic incident that made the Punisher who he is, or has Frank Castle always been this way?

Readers would get a chance to make their own minds up when the Punisher got his own comic series in the '80s.

In it, he took on everyone, from villains such as the Kingpin, to other superheroes such as Daredevil, who of course hated and fought against The Punisher's brutal methods.

FIRST APPEARANCE AMAZING SPIDER-MAN #129 CURRENT STATUS ALIVE

23 THE THING

A creature infused with molten rock and a lovable enjoyment of clobbering, the Thing was always a fun hero.

First appearing in 1961, Ben Grimm was the pilot of a mission to the stars that ended with its team being exposed to that pesky cosmic radiation Marvel residents always seem to insist on larking about near. Upon crash landing back on Earth, the other three team members find themselves cosmically blessed with powers over fire, light and body, while Grimm is cursed with becoming a rock-hard, super-strong monstrosity, a source of much guilt, turmoil and strife for both Grimm and his Fantastic friends.

Still, whatever his appearance, the Thing is not just a gritty face. As time went on, Reed Richards – who ignored Grimm's warnings about cosmic rays and now blames himself for his condition – tries to find a cure for his friend. Yet, interestingly, Grimm starts to adapt to life as the Thing and even rejects a cure in the fear that blind sculptor Alicia Masters – who he had fallen for – wouldn't fancy him when he didn't look like a terrifying volcano-man.

Despite such problems, he does achieve human form several times throughout his career in the comics, including a period during the Secret Wars when a device allows him to switch from human to The Thing whenever he chooses.

FIRST APPEARANCE FANTASTIC FOUR #1 CURRENT STATUS ALIVE

22 SHADOWCAT/KITTY PRYDE

From her early days as the merry mutants' teenage recruit during Chris Claremont and John Byrne's early '80s *Uncanny X-Men*, Kitty Pryde has really grown as a character.

Able to phase through solid objects and even people, she made her debut in *Uncanny X-Men* #129 before becoming a fully-fledged team member in #139. Taking her name from a real-life classmate of Byrne's, Claremont's depiction of Kitty's bright personality was inspired by then-X-editor Louise Simonson's daughter Julie.

Modelled by the artist to resemble a young Sigourney Weaver, she valiantly defeated a N'Garai demon all on her own in #143. Adopting her trusty dragon Lockheed in #156 after he rescued her from the Brood, she continues to boast a psychic bond with the alien beast to this day. Presumed dead after becoming trapped inside a Breakworld space bullet in Joss Whedon's *Astonishing X-Men*, she is subsequently rescued by Magneto.

The *Avengers Assemble* director told *Wired* that writing her was a nerd fantasy fulfilled.

"I don't feel like I ever have to have another one like that. Just being able to bring back Kitty Pryde, to give Kitty a journey. Kitty was the mother of Buffy as much as anybody."

FIRST APPEARANCE UNCANNY X-MEN #129 CURRENT STATUS ALIVE

21 HAWKEYE

After making his first appearance as a villain in 1964, it didn't take Clint Barton long to shift to the good guys when he joined the ranks of Earth's Mightiest Heroes in 1965's *Avengers* #16. Over the years, the sharpshooter has been a regular member of Marvel's superteam, featuring in West Coast Avengers in the '80s, and more recently as the team leader of the covert Secret Avengers.

Married at one stage to erstwhile S.H.I.E.L.D agent Bobbi 'Mockingbird' Morse, he sacrificed himself in a space battle with the Kree only to later be brought back to life by the Scarlet Witch. Tony Stark asked him to become the new Captain America after Steve Rogers' apparent killing, but he instead assumes the guise of Ronin, leaving his old Hawkeye identity in Young Avenger Kate Bishop's capable hands until eventually reclaiming it in 2010.

On the big screen, Hawkeye was brought to life by Jeremy Renner in first *Thor* and then *Avengers Assemble*. He never enjoyed much success flying solo until Matt Fraction and David Aja began highlighting the grittier side of his character in 2012 and his burgeoning partnership with Kate, which saw the pair battling the very real-life threat of the devastating tropical storm.

Clint Barton is a guy who is so driven, that even on his day off, he has to go out and help people or he can't sleep at night.

FIRST APPEARANCE TALES OF SUSPENSE #57 CURRENT STATUS ALIVE

20 NIGHTCRAWLER

Kurt Wagner is the blue-skinned, Bavarian circus acrobat and X-Man, famously portrayed by Alan Cumming in the second of Bryan Singer's X movies.

With blue skin, three-fingered hands and a demonic face, Wagner can teleport. This is accompanied by a 'bamf' noise, a puff of red smoke and the smell of brimstone.

Nightcrawler was originally a demon booted out of hell. The writer pitched him to DC but the character was rejected.

When Cockrum joined Marvel, Nightcrawler became part of the second generation of X-Men along with his other characters, Storm, Colossus and Thunderbird, making their debut in *Giant-Size X-Men* #1 in 1975, written by Len Wein. These new 'international' characters reinvigorated the series, and although he didn't get his own book until 1985, Nightcrawler was popular and remained in the team for years.

Wagner became a light-hearted and fun-loving character, as well as something of a ladies' man.

Over time, greater prominence was given to Wagner's Roman Catholic religion, and he also became more introspective. It was also revealed in 2003 that he was the child of Mystique and the demonic Azazel.

Alas, poor Kurt died in 2010, while trying to save messiah child Hope from anti-mutant villain Bastion.

FIRST APPEARANCE GIANT-SIZE X-MEN #1 CURRENT STATUS DEAD

19 DOCTOR STRANGE

Where to begin with Doctor Steven Strange, sorcerer supreme and the Marvel Universe's most mystical of magicians? Created by the Stan Lee/Steve Ditko wonder team, and making his first appearance back in 1963, Doctor Strange was never your usual superhero.

A former neurosurgeon who learned the mystic arts deep in the Himalayas, he perhaps best embodied the spirit of the '60s with his seeking out of new knowledge in the east, deeply odd storylines and some astonishingly visuals.

"I adore Ditko's design and the trippy visuals that go with it," said Brian K Vaughan when he took over the miniseries *Doctor Strange: The Oath* in 2006.

"It's such a classic Stan Lee touch to make the Sorcerer Supreme a man with a background in science and logic. "My favourite panel from Doc's origin involves Stephen looking down at his trembling hands right after he crashes his sports car, knowing that he'll never again be able to perform surgery. How brilliantly tragic that this guy can cast any spell imaginable, but he's reminded of his own flaws every time he picks up a drink, and hears the ice cubes rattling inside the glass."

Powerful, unknowable and just a little bit frightening, we can't wait to see Benedict Cumberbatch in the forthcoming Doctor Strange movie.

FIRST APPEARANCE STRANGE TALES #110 CURRENT STATUS WEIRD

18 JEAN GREY

Where would the X-Men be without Jean Grey? Marvel's mutants would certainly have a much less interesting history, that's for sure. Jean has been so important to the X-Men that even the most casual of comics fan knows her life: her Omega level (ie pretty much unlimited) psychic powers, decades-long relationship with Cyclops (albeit with occasional Wolverine diversions) and mentoring by Professor X. She wasn't always the powerful mutant we know today though...

Beginning life as Marvel Girl, she might have been one of the founding members of the X-Men but she was also the most boring. But the key to Jean Grey's success, much like the X-Men in general, is that she has evolved over the decades. Today she's grown into a character with much more going on.

Of course, a lot of that began in the '80s. Since then, she's been a thoroughbred X-Men character, with the writers managing to inject Jean with enough killer kudos to keep her at the forefront of mutant society.

One of the most dangerous beings in the entire Marvel Universe, she's been a mass murderer, a mother, and has defeated death on numerous occasions.

Her big screen counterpart hasn't always been entirely successful. but she's about as complex and frankly frightening a character as there has ever been.

FIRST APPEARANCE X-MEN #1 CURRENT STATUS ALIVE (AMAZINGLY)

HULK

Marvel's big green smashing machine

First appeared: The Incredible Hulk #1
(published in May 1962 by Marvel Comics)

Hulk is another of Stan Lee's genius creations with artist Jack Kirby. Although he started off grey in colour, the character was quickly changed to the bright green that he's known for today. In the comics he's been both a hero and occasionally villain - his great strength but constant rage means that he's extremely dangerous. Indeed, at one point, Tony Stark and several other heroes (collectively known as the Illuminati) banished Hulk into space. One of Marvel's most famous and enduring characters, he's also conquered the small screen in the 1970s with The Incredible Hulk TV show being an enormous hit. There have been two Hulk feature films and he remains a key part of the movie Avengers line up.

ALLIES

Bruce has support from his sometimes girlfriend in Betty Ross (who later became the Red She Hulk), Amadeus Cho, and the other members of super-team the Defenders. These include Dr Strange, Namor and the Silver Surfer. Bruce also has a strong friendship with Tony Stark, who has worked to cure him of his mutations.

SECRET ORIGIN

Before he was Hulk, Bruce Banner was a scientist. He was supervising the detonation of an experimental gamma radiation bomb, but was accidentally caught in the blast while saving a clumsy teenager who had stumbled into danger. The radiation causes him to mutate into a terrifying monster: the Hulk! Now Bruce spends his days trying to keep the beast inside at bay - only unleashing him when the world is in danger and his fellow superheroes need to call on some brute force.

SKILLS AND POWERS

Hulk is stronger than even the toughest superhero, can leap so high and far that he's practically flying, and smash his fists together so hard it creates a deadly shockwave. Oh, and he's also so tough he's practically indestructible! No wonder Iron Man has to keep a specialist 'Hulkbuster' suit on standby, in case he ever goes rogue.

ENEMIES

General Thaddeus 'Thunderbolt' Ross is Hulk's most persistent opponent, and one with a personal connection - he is the father of Bruce's girlfriend, Betty Ross. He pursued Bruce for years, but was himself eventually transformed into the very thing he despised the most, becoming the Red Hulk (though he has recently lost his powers again). Another monstrous foe is the Abomination - KGB agent Emil Blonksy who deliberately recreated Bruce's gamma experiment and mutated into a terrifying beast with even greater strength than the Hulk.

HOW TO

MAKE YOUR OWN COMIC WITH PHOTOS

Follow our guide on how to make amazing comics and stories using just photos and your imagination

> ASSEMBLE THE AVENGERS!
>
> ?!
>
> CAPTAIN AMERICAN GETS WORD OF A MONSTER ON THE LOOSE.

MADE A COOL COMIC OF YOUR OWN?
Email your pictures to:
futurekids@futurenet.com

1
FIRST!
You'll need to download an app to your smartphone or tablet called Halftone 2 - it costs £2.29 but it's worth every penny.

2
GATHER YOUR MATERIALS
Toys and figures make for great photo subjects – especially if you can pose them. We've got some Avengers Funko Pops which will make it feel extra comic-y.

SET UP

To make it look extra cool you'll need to get some extra light – positioning a lamp helps with this. You can also use a computer screen to bring up photos for backgrounds.

Add some fun with **over 80** professionally designed **comic style stickers**

GET SNAPPING!

Start taking those photos, moving your figures into new positions for each one. If you've got a pet it will make for an excellent monster.

USE THE APP

Open up the app, pick a layout and start putting in your photos in the order you want. There are lots of speech bubbles and special effects you can use.

THE AVENGERS HEAR THERE'S TROUBLE IN THE CITY.

GO!

THIS CITY IS FULL OF TASTY HUMANS, I WILL EAT THEM ALL!

HOLD IT RIGHT THERE!

HA-?!

I'LL HAVE YOU FOR TEA!

AAAH!!

CHOMP

GASP!

SHE'S TOO STRONG! WE CAN'T FIGHT HER...

CRUNCH MUNCH

HOW WILL THE AVENGERS GET OUT OF THIS?!

FIND OUT NEXT TIME...

ENJOY THE FINISHED THING!

Once you're done you can save the image and it'll give it a paper effect, here's our final comic.

FLASH

DC's speedster has had a long history and several different incarnations...

First appeared: Journey Into Mystery #83
(published August 1962 by Marvel Comics)

Barry wasn't the first version of the Flash - that was Jay Garrick, created in 1940 by Gardner Fox and Harry Lampert. The series was cancelled in 1948 (when superheroes weren't as popular as they are now), but Jay still occasionally shows up from time-to-time in modern comics.

There's no doubting, however, that Barry is the most popular and enduring version of the Flash. Part of that is down to his longevity (he first appeared in 1956) and partly it's down to his heroic sacrifice in 1985's 'Crisis On Infinite Earths', where he died to save the universe.

With Barry out of the picture, his nephew Wally West took on the role of the Flash (he'd already had plenty of practice as Barry's sidekick, Kid Flash). Then, more than 20 years after his death, Barry returned to life (an unusually long time in comics, where characters usually die and come back to life almost immediately), cementing his position as the definitive take on the character. Today the Flash is arguably the most popular he's ever been, partly due to the Grant Gustin-starring TV series.

SECRET ORIGIN

When Barry Allen's brother was murdered, he decided to become a forensic scientist. One night, a freak bolt of lightning struck his lab and he was covered in a cocktail of chemicals that gave him the power to run at almost the speed of light.

ALLIES

There have been several sidekicks known as Kid Flash over the years, the most popular of which is Wally West. Flash is also a key member of the Justice League, alongside Batman, Superman, Green Lantern, Wonder Woman, The Atom and many more heroes.

SKILLS AND POWERS

He's really, *really* fast. In fact Barry can run so fast he can even pass through solid objects, like walls, as well as heal quicker than normal human beings.

ENEMIES

Captain Cold (Len Snart) is the leader of evil super team, The Rogues, and Flash's greatest enemy. Armed with a freeze ray and a twisted intellect, he has frequently proven to be a deadly opponent - although in recent years he has been known to join forces with the Justice League. Zoom is another speedster, but without Barry's moral code. Trickster (James Jesse) was a con man with a dark sense of humour. And Grodd was a super intelligent gorilla in a cape. No, seriously.

DOCTOR WHO

BBC ONGOING ADVENTURES OF THE NINTH DOCTOR

011

TITAN COMICS

MEET THE CREATOR CAVAN SCOTT

Cavan writes books and comics and has created brilliant stories for Doctor Who, Adventure Time, Skylanders and loads more

HOW DID YOU FIRST GET INTO WRITING COMICS?

The first comic I ever wrote was for Power Rangers. They needed a script written in just one day and so I jumped at the chance.

The Ninth Doctor on the run, with companions Rose and Captain Jack.

WHO IS YOUR FAVOURITE CHARACTER TO WRITE FOR?

I think it's the Doctor [from Doctor Who] as he's such fun. He can be funny, angry and really rude – and everyone loves him anyway. Well, everyone except for the Daleks, and the Cybermen, and the Weeping Angels, and...

WHAT'S THE MOST FUN PART OF BEING A COMIC WRITER?

Working with amazing artists. I love coming up with an idea and throwing it over to the artist to see what they come back with.

WHAT'S IT LIKE WHEN YOU SEE YOUR FINISHED COMIC IN THE SHOPS?

It's amazing! That's one of the most exciting part of creating comics, knowing that it's out there for people to read and enjoy. It's the best feeling in the world.

WHAT ADVICE WOULD YOU GIVE SOMEONE WHO WANTS TO GET INTO WRITING COMICS?

Don't wait for anyone to give you permission to make comics – just make them. Create your own characters and world, and have fun. But try hard to finish your stories. It's easy to start new ideas, but if you're going to make it as a writer, people have to know that you can see things through to the end.

WHAT'S THE SILLIEST IDEA YOU'VE HAD FOR A COMIC?

It has to be Guffzilla. Bananaman eats a radioactive banana and produces a monstrous fart that rips apart Beanotown!

WHO IS YOUR FAVOURITE SUPERHERO?

It has to be Superman. He may be super-powerful and come from a different planet, but he's always trying to be the best he can be, and treats everyone fairly. Plus, he shoots laser beams out of his eyes! I wish I could do that!

THE TOP 25 HEROES PART THREE...

17 GAMBIT

Kidnapped at birth, and brought up by the street thieves of Fagan's Mob, little Remy LeBeau certainly had a troubled childhood.

Nicknamed 'Le Diable Blance', aka the White Devil, he fell into the care of numerous pairs of nasty hands along the way.

On developing his signature telekinetic powers though, Gambit escaped and wandered the world, jumping from one ill-fated employer to another, finding his abilities – an intense superiority over kinetic energy, and a hypnotic charm – too powerful to handle.

As his powers began to overwhelm him, Gambit fell into even more bad company, including the appropriately named Mister Sinister. It was only when he joined the guild in issue #267 of Uncanny X-Men, and met the good of his kind (including his future long-term on-off love-interest Rogue) that he found a home.

Love him or hate him, there's no denying that Gambit's made an impact over the years.

FIRST APPEARANCE UNCANNY X-MEN ANNUAL #14 CURRENT STATUS ALIVE

16 DAREDEVIL

WHERE IS HE? WHERE IS HE HIDING--?

When young Matt Murdock is blinded by a radioactive substance, his other senses become heightened to a superhuman degree. Learning to control these senses he is able to see by using the sounds around him to create radar-like images of his surroundings.

Murdock may be sightless but he's not short of vision. Whether as a lawyer during the day or as Daredevil at night, he believes firmly in justice. Despite losing his parents as well as his sight, he refuses to give up, overcoming everything that comes his way.

Originally described as the 'sightless swashbuckler', Daredevil was created by Stan Lee and Bill Everett in 1964.

A pretty poor 2003 film starring Ben Affleck may have damaged the public's opinion of him, but Matt Murdock remains one of Marvel's key heroes, and the TV series is fantastic.

FIRST APPEARANCE DAREDEVIL #1 CURRENT STATUS ALIVE

15 CAPTAIN BRITAIN

Intended as the British equivalent of Captain America, Brian Braddock was created by Chris Claremont and Herb Trimpe in 1976 for a new weekly comic book from Marvel UK.

Twin brother to Betsy, the X-Men's Psylocke, Braddock was a scientist who, following a near-fatal accident, was offered powers by legendary wizard Merlyn. He is later revealed to be part of a group of similar heroes, all dedicated to upholding the laws of Britain.

Armed with a telescopic staff, he was given his powers by a mystical Amulet of Right worn around his neck.

At times in the comics, he has been unable to use his powers outside of the UK or has had to wear his costume constantly.

Integrated fully into the Marvel Universe in 1978, he is the only Marvel superhero to have been written by Alan Moore who, with Davis, turned him into a noble, but fragile warrior.

After heading up the British superhero team Excalibur for a number of years, Braddock enjoyed a revival with Paul Cornell's excellent Captain Britain And MI:13.

Following a stint with the Avengers, he's now heading up the Braddock Academy. One of the few characters to not have made it successfully to the big screen, we'd love a movie!

FIRST APPEARANCE CAPTAIN BRITAIN WEEKLY #1 CURRENT STATUS ALIVE

14 WONDER WOMAN

She is one of the most socially significant characters in the history of comic books: Wonder Woman, the warrior princess of the Amazons.

First appearing in 1942 at the height of World War 2, she was the creation of William Moulton Marston: writer, psychologist and key figure in the invention of the lie detector. Marston devised a hero who fought Nazis with a 'Lasso of Truth' and whose founding purpose was to educate a male audience in how women could be as powerful as men.

As times moved on, so did her potential as a strong woman fighting for justice and equality. In 1987, DC Comics' George Pérez, after researching Greek mythology and feminism, rehauled her character by moving her from World War 2 to the present day, making her a smart, strong hero and changing the tone of the artwork.

It was a change that would usher in a new, more enlightened era for Wonder Woman; one that, finally, would not only create a hero for women, but also deliver an icon for all those who've ever felt like they were never truly accepted.

She's perhaps best known for the long-running TV series of the 1970's starring Lynda Carter. However, she pops up in Batman vs Superman, ahead of a full Wonder Woman film in 2017.

FIRST APPEARANCE ALL STAR COMICS #8 CURRENT STATUS ALIVE

13 GREEN LANTERN (HAL JORDAN)

Hal Jordan first took to the skies in 1959's Showcase #22. A fearless test pilot for Ferris Aircraft, he was given his power ring after former Green Lantern for Space Sector 2814, Abin Sur, crashed to Earth.

A member of intergalactic police force the Green Lantern Corp, he has over the years been joined by several other human Lanterns including Guy Gardner, the stern John Stewart and brash '90s newcomer Kyle Rayner.

Jordan first joined the fold of the Justice League in its inaugural appearance in 1960's The Brave And The Bold #28 – and once again in 2011's Justice League – and he, or one of his fellow Emerald Knights, has long been a constant presence in DC's team.

In 1970, he teamed up with emerald archer Ollie Queen to tackle more earthbound issues. However, he also became the villainous Parallax in 1992's Zero Hour before later embodying the restless spirit of the vengeful Spectre.

Resurrected by long-time Green Lantern writer Geoff Johns in 2004's Green Lantern: Rebirth, Jordan remains the Green Lantern Corp's most pivotal member.

Ryan Reynolds brought a great energy to Hal in 2011's under-performing movie Green Lantern.

It remains to be seen whether the Deadpool actor will have a role to play in any future Justice League blockbuster.

FIRST APPEARANCE SHOWCASE #22 CURRENT STATUS ALIVE

12 DEADPOOL

THAT'S WHAT *THIS* IS FOR.

COME GRAB A BOTTLE!

The groundbreaking 'Merc with a Mouth' is a modern-day success story. Well, modern-ish, originating in 1991, but certainly a newcomer compared to the majority of Marvel's A-listers, most of which were created in the '60s.

Deadpool has risen through the ranks to become one of the modern day's defining comic characters. You really couldn't imagine him in any other era of comics either: an assassin with a murky, backstory and a healing power that makes him basically impossible to kill, he's a long way from, say, Captain America.

And yet, he's loved dearly. Deadpool books continue to multiply, and he inspires a huge devotion among fans. But why? Is it the antihero assassin stance, the attitude, or just that he's so different? We suspect it's a combination of the lot.

And boy, is he entertaining. There aren't many comic characters that are consistently, genuinely funny, but Deadpool? He surely takes the comedy crown. Throw in some serious fighting skills, and you've got an unstoppable combination.

"There's nobody like him," his creator Rob Liefeld said in 2010. "He's not crying about anything. He didn't lose his mommy and daddy outside a movie theatre. His planet didn't blow up. His parents didn't drown like Aquaman. His uncle didn't get shot like Spider-Man. He's a good-time superhero ninja."

FIRST APPEARANCE NEW MUTANTS #98 CURRENT STATUS ALIVE

11 JOHN CONSTANTINE

A s a magical manipulator who keeps to the shadows, John Constantine is not your average superhero. Almost from the moment he first appeared in Alan Moore, Rick Veitch and John Totleben's The Saga Of Swamp Thing in 1985, Constantine has not only interacted with big-shot capes like Superman and Batman but has used his spooky techniques to get the better of them.

"With Constantine, I don't know who I was thinking of," Moore told The Comics Journal in 1986. "I just wanted this character who knows everything, and knows everybody – really charismatic. Who knows nuns, politicians and bikers, who is never at a loss for what to do." Given his own title, Hellblazer, in 1988, he battled everything from the powerful demon Nergal, to voodoo shaman Papa Midnite and the spiteful spirit of his unborn twin in the form of the Golden Child.

Constantine finally died earlier this year when Hellblazer was cancelled after an impressive 25 years. In his place, a more youthful JC is casting his spell over the fresh pastures of the New 52

Played as a dark-haired American by Keanu Reeves in 2005's film version, he will hopefully be more faithfully realised in Guillermo del Toro's Justice League Dark movie that we hear is in the works in the near future.

SORRY TO INTERRUPT.

I'M SURE MY INVITATION GOT LOST IN THE POST, RIGHT?

FIRST APPEARANCE THE SAGA OF SWAMP THING #37 CURRENT STATUS ALIVE

10 RORSCHACH

B orn Walter Joseph Kovacs, Rorschach is the antihero at the heart of Alan Moore and Dave Gibbons' all-time classic, Watchmen. This uncompromising vigilante turns rogue after costumed heroes are banned.

Getting his name from the ever-changing Rorschach inkblot on his full-face mask, he proves to be the real engine of the story as he drives his now-retired colleagues to look further into the murder of his former associate, the Comedian.

"If I had a favourite character to draw, the one that I'll draw is Rorschach," said Gibbons. "Basically you just have to draw a hat. If you can draw a hat, then you've drawn Rorschach. You just have to draw kind of a shape for his face and put some black blobs on it and you're done."

Rorschach eventually uncovers sinister genius Ozymandias' plot to save the world from nuclear extinction by faking an alien invasion, and pays for it with his life: Doctor Manhattan kills him to stop him exposing the plan.

"I didn't know Rorschach was going to die at the end of Watchmen until issue four," Moore said in 1988. "As I thought about it, I realised that there was no way he would compromise. And if he wouldn't compromise, he'd die!" The character was an instant hit with fans and was played to great effect by Jackie Earle Haley in Zack Snyder's 2009 film of the same name.

FIRST APPEARANCE WATCHMEN #1 CURRENT STATUS OBLITERATED

9 THOR

Thor is, of course, based on the God of Thunder from Norse mythology and was one of the founding Avengers.

The son of Odin and Gaea, Thor hails from Asgard and possesses superhuman strength, speed and agility. He wields the magical hammer Mjolnir which gives him the ability to summon storms and fly, as well as being an indestructible weapon. His enchanted Belt of Strength amplifies his strength and endurance.

Feeling his son needed a lesson, Odin sent Thor to Earth in the body of partially disabled medical student, Donald Blake, and without knowledge of his godhood. After discovering Mjolnir and foiling an alien invasion, he continued with his alter-ego, eventually falling in love with nurse Jane Foster and refusing to return home to Asgard.

"How do you make someone stronger than the strongest person?" said Stan Lee. "It finally came to me: Don't make him human – make him a god." Since then some of the biggest names in comics have worked on him. Proud, brave but often headstrong and arrogant, Thor is a natural opposite of his adoptive brother Loki.

Chris Hemsworth's cracking performance of Thor in a movie of the same name, as well as sequel *Thor: The Dark World*, and last year's *Avengers Assemble*, has also catapulted him back into Marvel's major league.

FIRST APPEARANCE JOURNEY INTO MYSTERY #83 CURRENT STATUS ALIVE

8 CAPTAIN AMERICA

...COME HAVE A CUP OF COFFEE WITH ME.

THE PLACE WE GO ALSO MAKES LATTES, IF YOU PREFER.

I DO.

Steve Rogers was the orphan of parents turned into a super soldier by an experimental serum created by scientist Abraham Erskine to help win World War 2. Although the experiment was a success, Erskine was assassinated without divulging the formula.

The serum gives him extreme strength, endurance, agility and healing abilities. Armed with a bulletproof boomerang-like shield, Rogers and his sidekick James 'Bucky' Barnes take on the Axis powers, including the Red Skull.

Created for Marvel Comics' predecessor, Timely Comics, by Joe Simon and Jack Kirby, the million-selling series debuted in 1941, a year before Pearl Harbour.

"We were always trying for new characters," Simon told a convention audience in 1998. "Captain America was a wartime thing, a patriotic thing, and we had the greatest villain you could think of: the Nazis and Adolf Hitler. It turned out, you put a little comedy into it, a very colourful costume, and it went over. It was not the first patriotic hero in comics but it was the best."

Reintroduced in the '60s, having been frozen in the Arctic, Rogers became a prominent member of the Avengers and one of Marvel's most popular characters.

Cap has been a regular at the movies since 1944, with Chris Evans the latest to don the costume in *Captain America: The First Avenger, The Winter Soldier*, and *Avengers Assemble*.

FIRST APPEARANCE CAPTAIN AMERICA COMICS #1 CURRENT STATUS ALIVE

7 HULK

Gamma rays have a lot to answer for. How many billions of dollars worth of damage has the Hulk caused over the years? We'd love to know, although we've no doubt that every single cent was worth it. Bruce Banner's raging alter-ego is a Marvel institution, a Jekyll and Hyde update who has managed to smash his way into our hearts.

"With the Hulk I thought it would be fun to get a monster and make him a hero," explains Stan Lee, of the green (though originally grey) giant's origins. "I always used to love the movie *Frankenstein*, but I always thought the monster was really the good guy. He didn't want to hurt anybody, but those morons with the torches were always running up and down the hills chasing him. So I thought I'll get a good monster. But just a good monster running around could get a little boring..."

A Lee and Kirby creation whose appeal has never diminished, Hulk is ridiculously powerful, hugely sympathetic and never less than entertaining. Icons don't come much brasher than the green giant, and his history is littered with superb storylines. He's been menace and saviour, a father, a husband, an intergalactic gladiator and a ruthless invader and is finally getting into the films he deserves thanks to the likes of *Avengers Assemble*.

He's a comic character who everybody in the world has heard of and loves.

FIRST APPEARANCE THE INCREDIBLE HULK #1 CURRENT STATUS GREEN

6 HELLBOY

His true name might actually be Anung Un Rama but comics fans know Mike Mignola's hornheaded supernatural investigator better as Hellboy.

The leading agent for the mysterious Bureau of Paranormal Research and Defense, the first Hellboy miniseries **Seeds Of Destruction** was published by Dark Horse in 1993. First summoned to Earth as part of a Nazi plot during World War 2, the stone-fisted semi-demon creature sided with the goodies.

Although he was spectacularly killed at the climax of 2011's **The Sound And The Fury**, death has proved to be no problem for the Great Beast, who is still going strong after two decades, although he is currently confined to his homeland in the ongoing **Hellboy In Hell**.

An big fan of Mignola's work, **Pacific Rim** director Guillermo del Toro made the character the focus of two feature films in 2004's **Hellboy** and 2008's even better sequel **The Golden Army**.

Del Toro cast his regular lead actor Ron Perlman in the part, believing the **Sons Of Anarchy** actor was perfect: "Hellboy's a guy you could hang out with... Then all of a sudden he has to go out and kick some monsters"

Sadly, plans for the third and final part of the trilogy appear to have fizzled out at the time of writing. Hopefully Hollywood will see sense and we'll get another Hellboy movie..

FIRST APPEARANCE SD COMIC-CON COMICS #2 CURRENT STATUS IN HELL

WORLDS OF WONDER

**As every comics fan knows, there's more than one Earth.
Here are just a few of the many Earths in Marvel's multiverse...**

THE BASIC WORLDS

EARTH-616

FIRST APPEARS: MOTION PICTURE FUNNIES #1

The basic Marvel universe. Unless otherwise specified, all events that happen in Marvel comics take place here.

EARTH-2301

FIRST APPEARS: MARVEL MANGAVERSE #1

This is where the stories in Marvel Mangaverse are set. It features familiar characters, but drawn in a manga style. Simple.

EARTH-1610

FIRST APPEARS: ULTIMATE SPIDER-MAN #1

The 'Ultimates' universe, where retooled versions of Marvel's characters exist. Miles Morales is Spider-Man and the Avengers are known as the Ultimates.

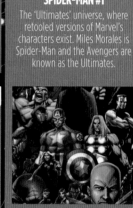

PARALLEL WORLDS

EARTH-1218

FIRST APPEARS: NEW EXILES #3

The 'real' world. That's us. Superheroes are just characters on the printed page and cinema screen and no one has any special powers. Boring!

EARTH-26

FIRST APPEARS: DARK REIGN: FANTASTIC 4 #2

Reed Richards prevents the superhero civil war – by building a machine that gets rid of everyone's superpowers. Well, that's one way to do it!

EARTH-552

FIRST APPEARS: EXILES #86

In this universe, Galactus is a healer who restores life to dead planets, rather than wiping them out. However Norrin Radd, the Silver Surfer, turns against him.

EARTH-666

FIRST APPEARS: SECRET AVENGERS #33

Earth's population is made up of undead beings, including vampires, werewolves and mummies. However, a band of heroes gets together to form the Avengers of the Undead.

EARTH-772

FIRST APPEARS: WHAT IF? VOL 1 #1

In this universe, the Fantastic Four are actually the Fantastic Five, as Spider-Man joins Reed Richards and the gang. Susan ditches Reed for Namor and the FF break up.

EARTH-998

FIRST APPEARS: X-MAN #63

Nate Grey (aka X-Man) stumbles upon this world where America was ruled by Red Queen (Madelyne Pryor) from her floating city, with support from the villainous Mr Scratch.

EARTH-295

FIRST APPEARS: X-MEN VOL 2 #41

The 'Age Of Apocalypse' universe. Legion travels back in time and accidentally kills Professor X, forcing Magneto to lead the X-Men against the immortal Apocalypse.

EARTH-9250

FIRST APPEARS: WHAT IF? VOL 2 #37

In this unfortunate reality, Wolverine becomes 'Lord of the Vampires' and leads a team of X-Vamps, eventually killing the Punisher!

EARTH-58163

FIRST APPEARS: HOUSE OF M #1

The 'House of M' universe. Here, Magneto has been made leader of the world's mutants and normals have become a despised underclass.

EARTH-231

FIRST APPEARS DARK REIGN: FANTASTIC 4 #3

The Fantastic Four's Reed Richards meets Doctor Strange, Namor, Black Bolt and Iron Man. And, er, goes ahead and kills them to stop them from becoming too ambitious.

EARTH-45828

FIRST APPEARS: HYPERKIND #1

The Razorline universe created by horror writer Clive Barker. Four series – *Ectokid, Hokum & Hex, Hyperkind* and *Saint Sinner* – ran between 1993 and 1995 before the series was closed.

DARK WORLDS

EARTH-267
FIRST APPEARS: AVENGERS #267
Marvel villain Kang sparks a nuclear war that wipes out the Earth, leaving him as the only survivor – until he is killed himself. Bleak.

EARTH-597
FIRST APPEARS: EXCALIBUR #6
This is the Marvel world where that alternative history cliché came true: the Nazis won World War 2.

EARTH-744
FIRST APPEARS: MIGHTY WORLD OF MARVEL VOL 2 #13
George Smith is Captain Airstrip One – aka this universe's version of Captain Britain – in this world, clearly inspired by George Orwell's famous novel, *1984*.

EARTH-952
FIRST APPEARS: WHAT IF? VOL 2 #70
The Silver Surfer decides to stick by Galactus and the Earth is consumed. The Fantastic Four survive, but become Heralds of Galactus themselves. Ouch.

EARTH-2149
FIRST APPEARS: ULTIMATE FANTASTIC FOUR #21
The Marvel Zombies world. Extremely close to Earth-616 with one nasty difference: zombies! A virus turns many of our favourite heroes into flesh-eating monsters.

EARTH-811
FIRST APPEARS: X-MEN #141
The 'Days Of Future Past' universe. The X-Men fail to prevent Senator Kelly being killed, leading to a timeline where mutants are held prisoner in concentration camps, and robots rule America.

EARTH-9591
FIRST APPEARS: RUINS #1
If something bad could happen, then on this world it did. Peter Parker's spider bite mutated him horribly, Bruce Banner became a nasty mess. Even Galactus was dead. Oh dear.

EARTH-42777
FIRST APPEARS: EXILES #23
Everyone loves Tony Stark, right? Not on this world. Here he's forced the world into electing him Emperor of the Planet, while killing any superheroes who oppose him.

ON-SCREEN WORLDS

EARTH-96283
FIRST APPEARS: SPIDER-MAN
The Sam Raimi universe. The Spidey movie trilogy takes place here. Peter Parker can shoot web-fluid from his wrists, and he meets Gwen Stacy after already dating Mary Jane.

EARTH-58470
FIRST APPEARS: HOWARD THE DUCK
George Lucas' terrible *Howard The Duck* movie takes place on this awful world. Where's Galactus when you need him, eh?

EARTH-10005
FIRST APPEARS: X-MEN
The X-Men movies happen on this Earth. Mutants exist, but no other superheroes have been encountered. Games *X-Men: The Official Game* and *X-Men Origins: Wolverine* also take place here.

EARTH-199999
FIRST APPEARS: IRON MAN
The Marvel Cinematic Universe, where the Avengers films take place. Hulk looks like Ed Norton and then Mark Ruffalo and the Mandarin is very different…

EARTH-400005
FIRST APPEARS: THE INCREDIBLE HULK
The fondly-remembered '70s Hulk TV series, where a wandering Bill Bixby helps people, before transforming into a pasty-green Lou Ferrigno in ripped shorts.

EARTH-26320
FIRST APPEARS: BLADE
The three Blade movies take place here. Given Marvel has recently reacquired the character's film rights, however, it seems unlikely that a potential fourth film would be in the same place and time.

CROSSOVER WORLDS

EARTH-7642
FIRST APPEARS: SUPERMAN VS THE AMAZING SPIDER-MAN #1
Ever wondered who'd win in a fight between Superman and Spider-Man? This is the place to find out, as here, Marvel and DC characters live together.

EARTH-5556
FIRST APPEARS: DOCTOR WHO WEEKLY #1
For many years, Marvel UK published Doctor Who comics alongside other titles like *Death's Head*. Ooh, the possibilities…

EARTH-120185
FIRST APPEARS: TRANSFORMERS (UK) #9
Marvel UK's much-loved *Transformers* comic takes place on this Earth, and shared the planet with the characters of *Action Force* (the UK version of *GI Joe*).

EARTH-818793
FIRST APPEARS: MARVEL ZOMBIES VS ARMY OF DARKNESS #2
The universe of the *Evil Dead* movies. Ash (as played by Bruce Campbell) is transported from here to the Marvel Zombies world.

BIZARRE WORLDS

EARTH-82801
FIRST APPEARS: WHAT IF? #34
The bananaverse. The Fantastic Four's powers are all fruit-derived. No, really. Sue Storm's banana is invisible, of course.

EARTH-1228
FIRST APPEARS: WHAT IF? #11
The Skrulls send a box of cosmic rays to the Marvel offices, which transforms Stan Lee, Jack Kirby, Sol Brodsky and Flo Steinberg into the Fantastic Four. Weird.

EARTH-8311
FIRST APPEARS: MARVEL TAILS #1
Homeworld of Peter Porker, the spectacular Spider-Ham, Ant Ant, Goose Rider and Crayfin the Punter. Basically, your favourite Marvel character as an animal.

EARTH-8101
FIRST APPEARS: AMAZING SPIDER-MAN FAMILY #1
The Monkeyverse, as seen in *Marvel Apes*. All of your favourite heroes and villains are here, but they're all monkeys. I promise we're not making this up.

EARTH-21989
FIRST APPEARS: MARVEL TALES VOL 2 #219
And here's the X-Babies universe… We do like Magneto's gang being the Brotherhood Of Mutant Bullies though.

TOP 10 VILLAINS!

Where would our heroes be without villains?
We count down 10 of comics' meanest menaces...

#10 RED SKULL

A manic meanie with a face like angry death itself, Red Skull first appeared as a henchman in 1941's Captain America Comics #1. He was promptly defeated, only to rise again – many, many times since then!

#09 VENOM

A grotesque mirror image of Spider-Man, created for our hero's 25th anniversary. Venom is a simple character, but loud and brash when it comes to facing his big rival.

#08 GALACTUS

A high-point of early Fantastic Four issues was the arrival of the ultimate bad guy. Galactus is a cosmic entity in the body of a giant, who once drained the energy from living planets. Booo!

#06 GREEN GOBLIN

Spidey's nemesis is a gangland boss with a mysterious secret identity and spooky look. His alter-ego has changed over the years – at first he was Norman Osborn, father of Peter Parker's best friend Harry!

#07 LOKI

Since Thor began in the 1960s, Loki has been a constant menace – sharp-tongued and charming, quick to deceive and willing to betray. What a swine.

#05 ULTRON

An indestructible robot who's been battling The Avengers for nearly 50 years. Ultron has simple (if gross) aims: destroy humanity. In the last Avengers film he took over all of Tony Stark's robots and used them against him!

#04 LEX LUTHOR

A cocky criminal with no powers, Lex has always been the perfect enemy for Superman – the sly guy who pretends to side with the average man or woman by putting brains over brawn.

#03 MAGNETO

Magneto made a strong initial impression in the first issue of the X-Men's book, establishing himself as the wicked flipside to Professor X. Later, Magneto became a sort-of hero, and he even ran the X-Men for a bit, which seems mad now!

#02 DOCTOR DOOM

Paranoid, looking for vengeance against a world that doesn't value him, Doom reminds us of every best friend gone bad. He's the noble bad guy who could have been a hero but just can't get over his Fantastic Four envy.

DOOM WHO PULLS THE STRINGS.

#01 THE JOKER

The joy of the Joker is he can be played many ways: as a simple goon, or a super-evil thug, or someone insane who can switch from clownish to deadly in the blink of an eye. Between 1940 and 1956 he was in the Bat-books virtually every month, though no reader from the period would recognise him now. Whenever an innocent gets hurt, or bad things happen to good people, we can picture Batman's über-villain giggling away – unaware that comeuppance is coming soon!

BORN TO BE BAD

Where would our heroes be without villains? We take a look at 20 of comics' meanest menaces...

Without their wickedness, Peter Parker would be left swinging around Manhattan, while Clark Kent would twiddle his thumbs in an empty *Planet* newsroom. Wrong-headed and vicious they may be, but at least the bad guys of comics give our heroes something to do.

Here then are 20 of our favourite villains. You might not agree with every choice, naturally, but that's bad guys for you; it's their job to be a nuisance.

#20
KINGPIN

As a Spider-Man villain in the late '60s, Wilson Fisk was definitely of the second tier – a chubby gangland boss. But Fisk became the undisputed ruler of the New York underworld. In storylines like 'Born Again', he became Marvel's most compelling villain.

FIRST APPEARANCE **AMAZING SPIDER-MAN #50, JUL 1967**

#19
RA'S AL GHUL

He's a rare supervillain, this 'demon's head' – a kinda dashing, globe-trotting assassin. Ra's eco-terrorist ways combined with the fact that he appears to be Batman's equal and his daughter Talia is one of the few who might steal Bruce Wayne's heart, makes him one of DC's most complex baddies for the Caped Crusader.

FIRST APPEARANCE **BATMAN #232, JUN 1971**

#18
DARK PHOENIX

The reason the original Dark Phoenix story worked so well was not the supreme power on display, but that this was our friend, nice girl Jean Grey, gone off the rails. It's the greatest corruption/fall/redemption tale in comics – endlessly referenced and revived (but for once that's alright: it's in the name).

FIRST APPEARANCE **X-MEN #134, JUN 1963**

#17
MR MXYZPTLK

One of comics' most Marmite villains: an impish, powerful magical trickster from the '5th Dimension', almost impossible to stop unless you get him to return home (usually by tricking him into saying his own name backwards). More interested in tormenting Superman than anything else.

FIRST APPEARANCE **SUPERMAN #30, SEP 1944**

#16
BRAINIAC

There are lots of different Brainiacs, but most appear as green humanoid alien androids with no shortage of evil plans; he's the ideal bad guy for when Lex seems a little bit too boringly human.

FIRST APPEARANCE **ACTION COMICS #242, JUL 1958**

#15
POISON IVY

Strong female villains are a rarity, and those there are, are usually predictable assassins. Poison Ivy is different: her extreme brand of eco-terrorism making her one of those bad guys who, for all their craziness, just might turn out to be on the right side after all.

FIRST APPEARANCE **BATMAN #181, JUN 1966**

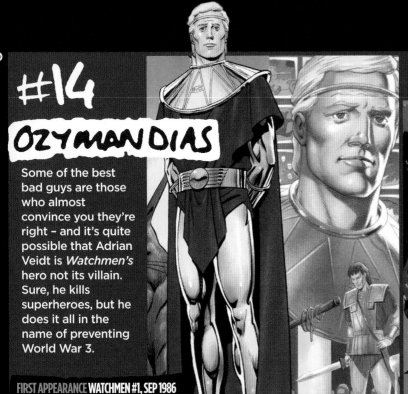

#14 OZYMANDIAS

Some of the best bad guys are those who almost convince you they're right – and it's quite possible that Adrian Veidt is *Watchmen's* hero not its villain. Sure, he kills superheroes, but he does it all in the name of preventing World War 3.

FIRST APPEARANCE **WATCHMEN #1, SEP 1986**

#13 CATWOMAN

Catwoman ('The Cat' when she first appeared in 1940) began as one of the boys. No troubled soul but purely in the game for cash and giggles; these days her motives are murkier, but her delightful don't-give-a-damn-what-people-think attitude remains.

FIRST APPEARANCE **BATMAN #1, SPRING 1940**

#12 TWO-FACE

One of the earliest Bat villains (first seen in 1942), and consistently amongst the most compelling: a clean-cut, well meaning good guy sent crazy when half his face is scarred by acid, Harvey Dent becomes a crime boss who chooses to be good or evil on the flip of a coin.

FIRST APPEARANCE **DETECTIVE COMICS #66, AUG 1942**

#11 ULTRON

An indestructible robot, developed and rebuilt in obsessive bouts of self-improvement, Ultron has simple aims: destroy humanity. He's got a great face, a chilling attitude and is currently to be found bothering most of the Marvel Universe in the ongoing 'Age Of Ultron' event.

FIRST APPEARANCE **AVENGERS #54, JUL 1968**

10 RED SKULL

A manic Nazi with a face like angry death itself, Red Skull first appeared as Hitler's agent in 1941's *Captain America Comics* #1 – and was promptly killed off, only to rise again once Timely Comics realised that here was villain gold. He's returned to trouble the modern era many times, not least when wielding the reality-warping Cosmic Cube.

FIRST APPEARANCE **CAPTAIN AMERICA COMICS #1, OCT 1941**

#9 VENOM

In the late '80s a new generation of creators were making a name for themselves, led by Todd McFarlane on *Spider-Man*. McFarlane upped the violence and added Venom. Created for Spidey's 25th anniversary, this mutation of the dramatic black 'alien costume' now appeared as a rabid monster. Venom's a simple character, but these were loud, brash times – and it made a huge impact.

FIRST APPEARANCE AMAZING SPIDER-MAN #299, APR 1988

#8 GALACTUS

A high point of early *Fantastic Four* issues was the arrival of the ultimate bad guy: effectively, this time the FF went up against God. Galactus is a cosmic entity in the body of a giant, who existed only to drain the energy from living planets. The first 'Galactus Trilogy' gave comics an epic sweep like nothing before it, or possibly ever since.

FIRST APPEARANCE FANTASTIC FOUR #48, MAR 1966

#7 LOKI

Since Marvel's *Thor* began in the early '60s, Loki has been a constant menace; sharp tongued and charming, quick to deceive and willing to betray. But, as family, he's rarely exiled completely. Though physically powerful, Loki ususally tries to instigate battles between others.

FIRST APPEARANCE JOURNEY INTO MYSTERY #85, OCT 1962

GREEN GOBLIN #6

Doctor Octopus was Peter's earliest 'Big Bad', but was soon replaced by the Green Goblin, a gangland boss with a mysterious secret identity and a spooky, Halloween-themed look. It was revealed that he'd really been Norman Osborn – father of Peter's best friend – all along. Norman would go on to kill Peter's girlfriend, Gwen, in one of the most shocking comic book stories of all time.

FIRST APPEARANCE AMAZING SPIDER-MAN #14, JUL 1964

#5 DARKSEID

He exists in a nether-world, in the DC universe but not of it. Granite-of-face, Darkseid (you say it like 'dark side') is a grim space-god who rules the industrial wasteland of Apokolips, a flame-belching depiction of a mucked-up Earth – our future. This is an individual absorbed in an insane quest for control, a mission that reveals deep cowardice and character flaws.

FIRST APPEARANCE SUPERMAN'S PAL, JIMMY OLSEN #134, NOV 1970

#4 LEX LUTHOR

He has no superpowers and in many ways is like a crude mad scientist stereotype, but Lex Luthor has greatness in him. Luthor's always been the perfect enemy for Superman, that alien who sides with the common man. Not because he's as strong - but because he's smarter, richer and he has the establishment on his side. Lex is every greedy businessman in one man. His career has even seen him serve as US president!

FIRST APPEARANCE **ACTION COMICS #23, APR 1940**

#3 MAGNETO

Magneto made a strong initial impression in the first iss of the X-Men's book, establishing himself as the wicked flipside to Professor X. Later, Magneto would become a sort-of hero; under writer Chris Claremont he got softer leading to times even running the X-Men, ruling a mutar nation, and losing and regaining his powers numerous times. Magneto's depth makes other villains seem thin and weedy.
Ans has there ever been a better film baddie than Magneto as portrayed by Sir Ian McKellen in the many X-Men movies?

FIRST APPEARANCE **X-MEN #1, SEP 1963**

#2 DOCTOR DOOM

Victor Von Doom's creation was deliciously simple – Stan Lee saw him as an evil mirror image of Reed Richards. The explosion that scarred him came from experiments to contact the dead but Doom's decision to become a self-imposed 'Man in the Iron Mask' has never wavered. Kirby said, "He's a good-looking guy, and he only has a tiny scar on his cheek, but because he's such a perfectionist he can't bear to see that imperfection." He's the noble bad guy who could have been a hero but, alas, that fatal flaw...

FIRST APPEARANCE **FANTASTIC FOUR #5, JUL 1962**

#1
THE JOKER

The joy of the Joker is he can be played many ways: as an over the top joke; as a killer thug (early comics saw him as a regular ganglord); and as something insane that can switch from delightful clown to deadly murderer in the blink of an eye. Only a last-minute decision allowed the Joker to survive the comic *Batman* #1. He appeared in two stories that issue, and the end of the second was swiftly reworked to save him, at the request of editor Whitney Ellsworth.

Between 1940 and 1956 he was in the Bat-books virtually every month, though no reader back then would recognise the modern, more crazy version of the films or even the TV series. Today, every time an innocent dies, or bad things happen to good people, we can picture *Batman*'s most famous villain, a giggling reminder that life can be random and vicious and very, very unfair.

FIRST APPEARANCE **BATMAN #1, SPRING 1940**

STAR WARS COMICS

Loved The Force Awakens and want more? Try these comics!

We've watched the latest Star Wars movie five times now, and the next one, Rogue One, is nearly here! We don't want to wait that long without seeing more of Finn, Rey, Poe and BB-8, but thankfully there are loads of great Star Wars: The Force Awakens comics to tuck into. Some tell stories of the characters before the film, and others are retelling the film itself from a new angle. If you want more from Star Wars you should definitely check all of these out...

SHATTERED EMPIRE

This comic covers the events between Star Wars Episode 6 and 7 and follows Luke and Leia Skywalker, Han Solo, Chewbacca, Lando Calrissian and the parents of Poe Dameron - Shara Bey and Kes Dameron - after the Battle of Endor in Return of the Jedi. It focuses on the retrieval of two very special plants - fragments of the Tree that once grew at the heart of the Jedi Temple.

STAR WARS: THE FORCE AWAKENS

This one is the comic book version of the film and follows the same story - from Rey and Finn on Jakku to the amazing fight with Kylo Ren on Starkiller Base. It's not quite the same as the film so it will be great to read a slightly different version.

OUT NOW

POE DAMERON

The best pilot in the resistance has got his own spin-off comic series that looks at what Poe and BB-8 were up to before The Force Awakens. Expect some amazing flying and fights with the evil First Order as they look for the first clues to Luke Skywalker's location.

VOL 1-4 **OUT NOW**

HAN SOLO

Before The Force Awakens, Han Solo was a famous smuggler and this comic shows off what he was like before he properly joined the Rebellion. It's set between films 4 and 5 and he's torn between his old life and the rebellion while he's on a mission to uncover spies during a huge spaceship race. Will he catch the spies or abandon his mission so he can win the race?

OUT NOW

C-3PO : THE PHANTOM LIMB

You don't get to see much of C-3PO in The Force Awakens movie, but he's got a really impressive history from the previous films. He used to be completely gold with this comic telling the story of how he got his red arm in this film. It gets really emotional.

OUT NOW

Oh wow! It's your TOP
SPIDER-MAN

Everything you need to know about everybody's favourite Marvel hero

1

Spider-Man (and his secret identity Peter Parker) were created by editor Stan Lee and artist Steve Ditko all the way back in 1962!

2

Spidey was different to most superheroes at the time – while others were usually grown-ups, he was a teen, with problems young readers could relate to.

3

One early comic featured a shocking twist: Peter's girlfriend Gwen Stacy was accidentally killed when Spidey tried to save her from th Green Goblin.

FACTS!

5

There are currently two Spider-Men in the comics! Peter Parker wears the famous red suit, but Miles Morales has taken on the role of protector of New York, and wears a black suit.

ON SCREEN

Tobey Maguire played Peter Parker in 2001's Spider-Man. It had two sequels and was then rebooted in 2012 as The Amazing Spider-Man with Andrew Garfield as the lead. Mostly recently Tom Holland's taken on the role for Marvel's Captain America: Civil War!

SPIDER-MAN LOVES

★ Photography
★ Mary Jane Watson
★ Cracking jokes

4

In 2007's Civil War comic, Peter Parker sensationally revealed his secret identity to the world, risking his life in the process.

TOP 5 ENEMIES

Doctor Octopus

The Green Goblin

The Lizard

Venom

Kraven the Hunter

5

IRON MAN

First appearing in a 1963 comic, *Tales Of Suspense* #39, comic legend Stan Lee, with a script by Larry Lieber, introduced us to a superhero who wasn't born from falling into a vat or being bitten by a spider. Instead, Tony Stark is a normal man who is caught behind enemy lines: injured by a Vietnamese booby trap, Stark escapes after secretly building an indestructible suit of iron.

As the world experienced real-life wars – from Korea to Vietnam, the Gulf to Afghanistan – the Tony Stark origin story has changed. Yet what hasn't altered is that this is a hero whose secret and super identities are just as interesting and important as each other. Iron Man may have been able to fly and blow stuff up, but Tony Stark's mind – boosted, of course, by huge wealth – was his true superpower. And it was a mind, as wisecracking and cocky as it may be, that also held his darker side. Initially, his problems were summed up by his heart, which had been broken by his awful time as a captive, but later writers would add further layers to this back story.

Stark may have started out as an inventor, wanting to protect America's best interests, but from 1978, under writers David Michelinie and Bob Layton, his character would develop into something much more dark, deep and complex. Beyond the iron suit, Stark began to question the morality of his work. He was changed into a vulnerable, wounded figure who had plenty of personal problems.

In one famous story, after an incident when Iron Man's armour goes wrong and kills an ambassador, we see the Avengers (the superteam he founded), his butler Jarvis and the whole world lose faith in him.

That story sums up not only what's so interesting about the character Tony Stark – the real villain is himself – but also the elements that make him such a genuinely brilliant superhero: Beneath the impenetrable armour, there's a human being with as many flaws as the rest of us.

Of course much of Iron Man's recent success has been due to being played by the supremely cool Robert Downey Jr. And there seems to be no end to the ways in which Hollywood can explore this cool, conflicted character in the movies.

And thank goodness. Because we can't get enough of Iron Man.

FIRST APPEARANCE TALES OF SUSPENSE #39 CURRENT STATUS SWAGGERING

WOLVERINE

olverine is amazing! A cigar-chomping, adamantium-clawed Canuck who arrived as a small character in the X-Men, but quickly made a home for himself in the hearts of Marvel fans everywhere. Even before Hugh Jackman made Logan his own in the movies, every superhero fan knew exactly who was the coolest character in comics.

But why? Is it the attitude? The claws and healing power combo? Or perhaps it just comes down to sheer personality paired with the best sideburns of anyone, anywhere. Really, it's not difficult to understand the appeal of this particular X-Man.

Quite simply, he's the best at what he does: taking down villains and bringing an unstable, animal element to the X-Men.

From his very first appearances – in comics Incredible Hulk #180 and #181 in 1974 – something about Wolverine was just... different. All the elements that we've come to know and love were there right from the off.

Unlike so many of his mutant mates, Wolverine is not God-like. He's human, very much so, and if he's going to kill you, he's going to get right up in your face to do it.

As one of Marvel's most popular characters, he's had some amazing treatment on the page. The mystery-solving Origin miniseries gave us Logan's surprising backstory, Writer Frank Miller took him to Japan and Mark Millar examined his future in Old Man Logan. Much-loved X-Men scribe Chris Claremont changed the character into the man we know and love today, arguably more so than any other writer.

"My idea of Wolverine was that if you walked into his room, half of it would be a total trash heap, a sloppy couch and more beer cans than you can imagine, and half would be economy and grace – a stand for his sword and maybe a picture on a table," Claremont said.

A complex inner life, iconic character design and great writing have helped transform Wolverine into the superstar he is today. Unsurprisingly he was a massive hit in the X-Men series of films, and then the Wolverine spin-off movies thanks to Hugh Jackman's fantastic performance, but his finest moments are still to be found on the printed page, we reckon.

FIRST APPEARANCE **THE INCREDIBLE HULK #180** CURRENT STATUS **FIERCE**

"WOLVERINE IS NOT GOD-LIKE. HE'S HUMAN, VERY MUCH SO, AND IF HE'S GOING TO KILL YOU, HE'S GOING TO GET RIGHT UP IN YOUR FACE TO DO IT"

3

SPIDER-MAN

omic book fans might look up to the skies for Superman, or in a shadowy corner to find Batman, but if there's one superhero they can truly identify with, it has to be Peter Parker, your friendly neighbourhood Spider-Man.

Parker made his debut in August 1962 in the comic Amazing Fantasy #15, and casually changed the shape of superheroes forever. A clumsy, bespectacled teenage nerd, whose life is transformed after he is bitten by a radioactive creepy crawly, he was pure fanboy wish-fulfilment. Smart, strong and always quick with a witty line.

Apparently, former Marvel Comics editor Stan Lee came up with the idea for the wall-crawler after watching a spider climb a nearby wall.

Emphasising the famous line 'with great power there must also come – great responsibility!' the initially carefree Spidey is taught an important lesson after the burglar that he allowed to escape goes on to kill his Uncle Ben. The orphaned Peter's Aunt May is now the only family he has left, so he resolves to do the right thing from then on by doing battle with a host of colourful supervillains, from

Electro and the Lizard, to the Vulture and Doctor Octopus.

His greatest enemy, though, is surely the Green Goblin – Norman Osborn – who first fights ol' webhead in 1964's Amazing Spider-Man #14.

Peter's romance with the glamorous Mary Jane Watson has also been far from smooth. After getting married in 1987's Amazing Spider-Man Annual #21, their union was rubbed out after 2007's 'One More Day' storyline, when Peter struck a terrible bargain with Mephisto. But with the advent of the 'Brand New Day' era, MJ gradually slipped back into Pete's life.

While he's been rebooted many times in the movies (and is about to do so again), in the comics, things have taken a turn for the dark. Peter has apparently died, leaving his body now possessed by Doc Ock, who is trying to make amends for his former life of crime. "You can debate whether this version of Spider-Man is heroic or not," current Spidey writer Dan Slott says "But he thinks he's doing good and on paper there are a lot of things he's doing right." Whatever. Peter Parker, like Bruce Wayne, is far too big a personality to stay gone forever. One way or another, he'll be back!

FIRST APPEARANCE AMAZING FANTASY #15 CURRENT STATUS SORT OF DEAD, SORT OF NOT

"A CLUMSY, BESPECTACLED TEENAGE NERD, WHOSE LIFE IS TRANSFORMED, HE WAS PURE FANBOY WISH-FULFILMENT"

2

SUPERMAN

uperman is the original superhero. The template from which all later comic heroes were made from. Sure, before him there were others: the Shadow, the Phantom, the Spirit and so on, but Kal-El, last survivor of the planet Krypton, was the first to be truly... super.

He's got it all: the sad past, kindly parents in the form of the Kents, the secret identity and a whole host of enemies on his baddie list. Supes set the template for literally hundreds of heroes to follow, and the next 75 years (and counting) of comics. Even cool books such as Watchmen and Zenith are reacting against the ideas and character established by Superman authors Jerry Siegel and Joe Shuster.

The character's cool factor may shift from decade-to-decade – he was big in the '90s, but has spent the past 10 years or so languishing in the shadow of Batman – but he survives. Something about the Man of Steel means that he always comes back. He's not edgy and dark like Bruce Wayne, and he doesn't have the personal problems of Peter Parker, but somehow, we still can relate to this impossible man.

Superman kind of represents us at our best. He's an ideal, but he's also flawed enough to remain a compelling character that we root for.

The early stories pitch him as a tough guy fighter, and there are also plenty of occasions where he actually acts like a total fool. But what matters is that he keeps on trying to make things better, to help people, to save the day, no matter what.

The character is currently enjoying a great time in the comics with the astonishing All-Star Superman. Since then, the New 52 has been kind to the character, with Action Comics, Superman and Scott Snyder's Superman Unchained flourishing. On screen, Man Of Steel moved the film series out of the shadow of the older Christopher Reeve movies, creating an interesting, dynamic new look. Batman vs Superman didn't enjoy the critical acclaim many were expecting, but in his 75 years, Superman has been endlessly beaten, trapped, rebooted and even killed, yet he always finds a way to come back and save the day. Superman represents all of us striving for greatness. He gives us hope and reminds us that, for all our flaws, we too can be super.

FIRST APPEARANCE **ACTION COMICS #1** CURRENT STATUS **SOARING**

"SUPERMAN REPRESENTS US AT OUR ABSOLUTE BEST. HE'S AN IDEAL, BUT HE'S ALSO FLAWED ENOUGH TO REMAIN COMPELLING"

BATMAN

et's be honest, it's no great surprise that Batman is your top hero. Of course, a big part of his popularity is down to the huge success of Christopher Nolan's Dark Knight films, but even before then, comics fans knew precisely who was king of the superhero hill.

Call him the caped crusader, the world's greatest detective, the dark knight, or simply the Batman. This tough crime-fighter has been waging war on evil enemies for the past 74 years. He's older than most of us, and you can guarantee that – assuming humans survive that long, anyway – he'll still be doing so when we're all old and grey. He's a tormented hero (sometimes, anyway) with a dark past. Plus, he has the best base and a the best superhero car ever.

He's also the kind of superhero we all want to be. Who hasn't dreamed about being rich, mysterious and powerful at some point in their lives? Bruce Wayne has it all. And the best thing about the character? No superpowers. With hard work, we could be Batman. Well, maybe.

Actually, that's a bit of a fib. There are many geniuses, many top athletes and many brilliant detectives in our real world. But is there anyone out there who combines all these things, while also being a billionaire crime-fighter? Just like the equally loved Indiana Jones, all it takes is that tiny sliver of possibility to make us believe in him.

Like Superman, Batman has changed character quite a few times. He was a sinister figure lurking in the shadows in the very first issues; a playful, caring father to young Dick Grayson later on; a fun-lover living in the city; an underground freedom fighter in Frank Miller's wonderful Dark Knight Returns...

He's got the best line-up of villains too: Two-Face, Penguin; The Riddler; and, of course, the Joker - possibly the best baddie ever.

Of course he's had his fair share of stinkers. Batman vs Superman was roundly panned. And the less said about the Batman and Robin film the better. But Batman survives even those awful movies, because he's our way into a thrilling world of fantastic characters, life or death situations, laughter, tears and very cool costumes. And because of that, he's our number one hero!

FIRST APPEARANCE DETECTIVE COMICS #27 **CURRENT STATUS** ALIVE AND WINNING

"BRUCE WAYNE HAS IT ALL. AND THE BEST THING ABOUT THE CHARACTER? NO SUPERPOWERS. WITH HARD WORK, WE COULD BE BATMAN!"

CHILDREN OF

It's far and away the most potent idea the medium has thrown up, this school for 'gifted youngsters', this club for troubled teens coming to grips with their new powers...

The X-Men are mutants. They're *not* regular superheroes, who tend to be normal people gifted with strange abilities by magic or science. Instead they're a new sub-species, born different to us (and to each other), with strange physicality and abilities that usually become obvious in their teenage years. One will have wings, another can walk through walls – but these guys are the glorious ones, despite their oddity and outsider status.

Many, many more will have less enviable powers (secreting adhesive, say, or possessing a body composed of paraffin wax), and will inherit the consequent revolting appearances. Sometimes we meet those guys too.

The X-Men is a superhero team built of students and teachers from a special, secluded school where young mutants are taught how to use their powers; they come in all shapes and sizes, from every country and background, yet to the outside world they remain part of a larger, yet more secretive mass of mutant-kind. Regular folk know these guys are out there, somewhere, but they can't properly see them. As a consequence mutants are regarded, at worst, as enemies within – and, even at their very best, as figures of suspicion, never quite to be trusted.

In the real world, Batman – with all his resources and ingenuity – would have cleaned up Gotham City by now; Superman would have turned Earth into a paradise. But the X-Men have problems that will *never* go away, because they're part of what we are. The world – and the threats it

THE ATOM

contains – mutates around them, and the X-Men had better get their skates on, just to keep up.

THE FEAR FACTOR

It's easy to understand why regular people are rather scared of the X-Men – the general belief is that they're the next stage of humanity.

The early Marvel of the first years of the '60s was built on unhappy, alienated heroes – monsters like the Thing and the Hulk, teens like Spider-Man, men out of time like Captain America. But *X-Men*, when it was launched in 1963 – towards the end of Stan Lee and Jack Kirby's first Big Bang of inspiration – took this two or three stages further. Perhaps it went *too* far, for at first it wasn't a hit.

Why, though has never been quite clear. Maybe America wasn't quite ready for it? Perhaps it had too many characters, and it was unclear quite who we were meant to cheer for?

Not all of the early X-Men tales are memorable, it's true, but it's to Marvel's credit that this third team of superheroes – after the FF and then the Avengers, who debuted at

> ## "Regular folks know these guys are out there somewhere. But they can't see them..."

virtually the same time – should be so distinctly different to what went before.

One point of difference was immediately obvious; we had to learn about these heroes as their adventures went along, with nothing handed to us on a plate. Instead, we were thrown right into the middle of things, with the first action of *X-Men* #1 being the arrival of Marvel Girl to join an already existing team.

There was more mystery to these new guys, it was clear, and it wouldn't be for years – in a series of back-up stories that began in issue #38, in fact – that the entire background to the original X-Men would become clear.

But, though these were heroes we'd never seen before, we

understood them to a degree because they all had a unifying theme – they were the children of normal human parents, but born with strange powers or abilities. In many cases they'd managed to keep »

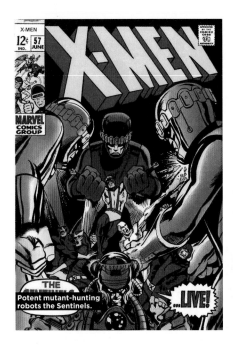

Potent mutant-hunting robots the Sentinels.

An early appearance of the Hellfire Club.

A new lease of life from Adams and Thomas.

Dave Cockrum cover to the 'Proteus' story.

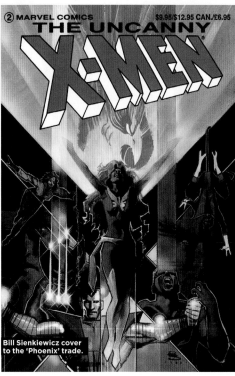

Bill Sienkiewicz cover to the 'Phoenix' trade.

these mutations secret, and now a small class of them were enrolled at a special, highly exclusive private school – one where the headmaster was secretly a powerful mutant, a guy dedicated to training these kids in their powers, and perhaps using them as the core of an army for some war ahead.

Beneath Professor Charles Xavier's school – at 1407 Graymalkin Lane in Westchester County, New York – lies the Danger Room, a huge, endlessly inventive mechanised training facility, and Cerbero, a giant computer that boosts Xavier's telepathic powers, allowing him to track new mutants all over the world. There are all the usual dorms and academic facilities, sure, but a hangar for the X-Men's aircraft too.

Time and again the X-Men must break from classes and rush into battle – to rescue some newly discovered or manifesting mutant, or to stop Magneto's schemes, as he plans a new, mutant-dominated world order from his bases on hidden asteroids or buried in Antarctica.

DANGER UNLIMITED
The first *X-Men* comics were full of surprises and fun – those inventive Danger Room death traps; Magneto's scheming; shy Cyclops burning with secret love for Marvel Girl as Angel and the others flirted happily with her – but though lasting characters cropped up (Blob, Mastermind, Quicksilver, Scarlet Witch) only a handful of issues are real classics.

Too often all the non-Magneto issues were weak and wobbly,

and – as a comic – *X-Men* survived in a lurching, way until the end of the '60s, when it peaked briefly with a spectacular-looking semi-reinvention by artist Neal Adams and writer Roy Thomas, before, at last, the book spluttered and died.

MAN OF STEEL
1975 was when it all changed, and *X-Men*'s swift march to its current position at – or nearly at – the very peak of comic book popularity began. The revival was as an international team, with only Cyclops, Professor X and the school background staying on, at least initially.

And though the old hands provided the continuity, and the

structure, the new guys were the stars: Storm, the Kenyan 'weather witch' with the shocking white hair; Colossus, Nightcrawler, and Wolverine.

Wolverine had originally been created as a Canadian enemy for the Hulk, but had appeared little since. Everyone could see his potential, though, and he soon became the spiciest ingredient in the new team's rich mix.

This new *X-Men* had, with its international cast, been designed to appeal to new world markets, but instead it was making an impact with non-traditional readers closer to home: women, teens, tough guys, old school Marvelites dragged back into comics by an exciting new take on old favourites.

Multi-lined mutants from the Jim Lee era.

A Barry Windsor-Smith X-Men love story.

The Danger Room in 'Days Of Future Past'.

Bad X-girls (and X-boys) gone good.

❝ Wolverine was soon the spiciest ingredient ❞

Along the way came new heroes – notably 13-year-old Kitty Pryde – and epic storylines with huge pay-offs, each jostling for space with a million ongoing sub-plots. With the likes of 'The Dark Phoenix Saga' and 'Days Of Future Past' – basis for an X-movie, of course – X-Men became the biggest noise Marvel had, and, even in these Avengers-centric times, continues to rule the roost.

Bad guys become good – and good guys bad – all the time in comics, but nowhere does this happen quite so often as in X-Men,

where Jean 'Marvel Girl' Grey once became the universe-threatening Phoenix, Beast has had his 'Dark' moments, Angel became leader of the Horsemen of Apocalypse, and Cyclops is currently being painted as one of the most complex, conflicted semi-villains in all Marvel.

Meanwhile, major villains have gone in the other direction: Wolverine, Rogue and Emma Frost started out as bad guys of one sort or another, while everyone from Sabretooth to Juggernaut

and Mystique has hung out with the team for a while. And then there's Magneto, the most layered and attractive villain in comics.

The X-Men's colours are blue and gold, but – as complex as the real world issues they reflect – most of their stories and characters are painted in uncertain shades of grey.

The X-Men has never been a story just about good guys and bad guys only – though both exist here – and it's that, perhaps above all, that makes X-Men matter so much more than other comic books.

Important X-Men
FIRST FIFTEEN

There have been many X-Men – about 90 at last count – but most of what really matters revolves around this core 15...

PROFESSOR CHARLES XAVIER
Unknowable, sometimes wheelchair-bound mentor; he owns the private school that's the team's base, funds and trains the young X-Men, but he often falls out with ex-pupils too. Played perfectly by Patrick Stewart.

CYCLOPS
Hyper-focused and serious-minded, Scott Summers is a brilliant leader and military tactician, and a force to be reckoned with himself, thanks to his powerful 'optics blasts'. One of those rare characters who can be either dull as ditchwater or utterly compelling.

MARVEL GIRL
Pretty red-haired telekinetic and, later, telepath, Jean Grey became the ultimate good-girl-gone-bad when she was reborn as Phoenix and later Dark Phoenix. Her descent was central to one of the X-Men's most compelling storylines ever.

BEAST
Strength and agility combined with real intelligence and learning made the Beast more than just the 'Thing, part two' that he was initially depicted as; his assorted blue-furred further mutations make him amongst the most intriguing of all of the X-Men.

ICEMAN
Honest, unlucky-in-love, emotionally (and physically) transparent 'little brother' of the original X-Men team, Bobby Drake was the Human Torch's freezing opposite, sliding around on roller-coasters of ice. Amazingly, his personality remains largely undeveloped after 50 years.

ANGEL
Eventual loser to Scott Summers in Marvel's first major superhero love triangle, handsome Warren Worthington III kept his magnificent wings hidden under regular clothes by means of a few cunning straps. Who knew the power of flight alone could be a big deal in the Marvel Universe?

WOLVERINE

Short, noble but aggressive – and almost impossible to hurt for long, this most macho of mutants became the most popular new superhero of the '70s, thanks to a mixture of cool, mystery, violence and charisma.

NIGHTCRAWLER

Kurt Wagner, light-hearted adventurer with the looks of a devil. He's a strong visual look and with clear potential for intriguing depth, he's been one of the more underused X-Men of recent years, surprisingly.

STORM

A real beauty, serene on the surface but as unpredictable as the weather she controls, Ororo Munroe is one of Marvel's two or three greatest female heroes. Independent, spiky and extremely capable.

COLOSSUS

This super-strong metallic giant – in reality humble Russian farmboy Piotr Rasputin – was initially expected to be the big star of the new X-Men, but nobody had quite anticipated the Wolverine effect...

KITTY PRYDE

Though her codename is Shadowcat, most know the early-teenage 'kid sister' X-Man by her regular name. Central to many of the great X-Men stories, she's the chatty equivalent to Buffy Summers.

ROGUE

With a badger-like shock of white in her hair, outrageous accent and intriguing powers, Rogue was one of the most successful later additions to the team.

PSYLOCKE

The Japanese ninja is actually a nice English girl at heart, Captain Britain's telepathic sister Betsy Braddock – this enduring X-Men character has become ever more important over the many years of the comic.

GAMBIT

Extremely popular attempt to replicate Wolverine's cool with a floppy-haired bad-boy thief, you love or hate Gambit. Some find his long coats, stick, card-throwing skills and accent completely laughable.

EMMA FROST

Emma 'The White Queen' Frost has been the most intriguing, entertaining addition to the X-Men line-up in years. The biggest danger with this girl is that she'll dominate every scene she appears in.

ENEMIES MINE

Over the years, the X-Men have fought everyone – other heroes, most recently! – but none keep coming back quite like these guys…

MAGNETO
One of the greatest of all comic book villains, he fights for mutant rights and survival in the most bullish of fashions.

BROTHERHOOD OF MUTANTS
First appearing as Magneto's followers, The Brotherhood has since been depicted as more of a mutant terrorist group.

JUGGERNAUT
An unstoppable physical force, and mystically gifted too, Cain Marko was introduced as a replacement for Magneto, but never quite made it.

SENTINELS
Perhaps the greatest creation of the X-Men books are their most powerful enemy – these giant, mutant-hunting robots.

APOCALYPSE
The great villain of the '80s was this extremely long-lived bruiser. His powers aren't that clear, and his motivations murky, but he proved popular nonetheless.

MR SINISTER
Mr Sinister was originally designed to be the frontman for the *real* bad guy: an apparently 11-year-old boy, who was ageing incredibly slowly. Weird!

HELLFIRE CLUB
Sebastian Shaw and Emma Frost had their starts in this Club, and the big 'Mastermind' reveal is one of the great *X-Men* moments.

CASSANDRA NOVA
The most potent (if confusing) new X-villain in decades: Charles Xavier's evil dark shadow, his sort-of twin sister…

THE BIGGEST BUST-UPS!

The *X-Men* titles are littered with great fights...

Nothing from the Grant Morrison or Joss Whedon runs? Afraid not – and it's not because we don't like them. The thing is, though genius, these two most individual takes on the X-Men were both built on *other* foundations: strange new twists, intriguing character interaction, big ideas and emotional beats. The fights, while very much there – and sometimes cool as hell – are simply not what we remember from those runs.

AGAINST MAGNETO | Uncanny X-Men #113
Shackled in Magneto's Antarctica base, the X-Men draw upon Storm's thief skills, then gather their wits for the showdown...

AGAINST PROTEUS | Uncanny X-Men #128
Moira McTaggert's super-powerful, reality-warping energy vampire son is running rampage across Scotland, and our heroes make their final stand.

AGAINST THE HELLFIRE CLUB | Uncanny X-Men #133
The X-Men defeated, a beaten Wolverine climbs out of the sewers for one unexpected final round with the Hellfire Club: he's small, he's bloodied, but he's sure not down. This is the moment that made Wolverine a star.

AGAINST THE IMPERIAL GUARD | Uncanny X-Men #137
One of the most celebrated issues of any comic ever. One by one the X-Men are defeated, until only Cyclops and a de-powered Marvel Girl are left – but then he's cut down, the psychic shackles shatter, and suddenly all bets are off...

AGAINST THE SENTINELS | Uncanny X-Men #142
The last remaining X-Men (Wolverine, Storm, Colossus, Magneto) make a final desperate assault on the enemy HQ, and are killed for their troubles. It was a genuine shock moment in one of the greatest ever X-stories.

AGAINST THE BROTHERHOOD OF MUTANTS | Uncanny X-Men #142
While the future X-Men fight a losing battle with the Sentinels, young Kitty Pryde – possessed by her future self – talks the early '80s team into a battle to save the future.

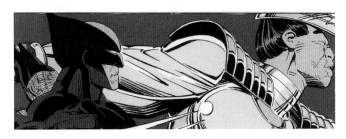

AGAINST SILVER SAMURAI | Uncanny X-Men #173
Wolverine battles have become one of the joys of X-Men comics, but perhaps the best is this scrap with retro-futuristic swordsman Silver Samurai.

AGAINST THE JUGGERNAUT | Uncanny X-Men #183
Wolverine stands to one side as Colossus takes a beating from the unstoppable Juggernaut in a pub brawl that destroys the very building they're drinking in.

QUIZ

Test your Spidey-sense with our Super Spider-Man Quiz!

So, how well do you know the web-slinging wall crawler and his adventures? Answer these 10 taxing questions to find out. Some of them are easy, and some are just a little bit trickier...

What is reptilian bad guy the Lizard's human name?

Name the fictional newspaper that grumpy J Jonah Jameson edits...

3 In which issue of Amazing Fantasy did Spider-Man first appear?†

4 How many robot tentacles does Doctor Octopus have?

5 What is the name of Peter Parker's school bully who later became a firm friend?

6 Which demon did Peter Parker make a bargain with to save Aunt May's life?

7 What sinister company did Norman Osborn co-found?

8 What is Peter Parker's middle name?

10 Finish this famous sentence from Spider-Man history: With great power there must also come great...

9 Who was Peter Parker's first girlfriend, before Gwen Stacey?

1) Dr Curt Connors
2) The Daily Bugle
3) #15
4) Four
5) Flash Thompson
6) Mephisto
7) Oscorp Industries
8) Benjamin
9) Betty Brant
10) "responsibility."

Tot up your correct answers and see how well you did below.

0-2   Hmm, not great. Get reading those comics...

3-4   Better, but you've still a way to go before you're an expert in Spidey...

5-6   Great work - you clearly know your Spider-Man!

7-8   Wow! Do you work for the Daily Bugle or something?

9-10   There's only one explanation... You *are* Spider-Man!

WORDSEARCH

CAN YOU FIND ME?

A	I	W	T	B	U	K	L	N	I
D	G	H	T	H	A	N	O	S	R
V	F	N	T	H	M	X	U	R	O
E	C	Z	K	U	L	T	R	O	N
N	I	K	O	L	S	T	W	H	F
O	A	E	P	K	L	I	G	T	I
M	M	B	G	T	P	F	N	P	S
Q	S	J	O	S	J	S	M	L	T
A	D	O	A	H	S	F	U	R	Y
G	P	W	G	R	O	O	T	K	S

Find the following words in the grid

HULK
THOR
LOKI
ULTRON
THANOS

VENOM
WASP
FURY
IRONFIST
GROOT

LIONHEART

N IS FOR

NUMBERS

We get our calculators out, and give you all the numbers that count in the world of superheroes!

904

Final issue of **Action Comics**' original run before 2011's New 52 reset

US $682,450,750

The total cost of being **Batman** in the Nolan trilogy, according to *Moneysupermarket.com*

4

Characters who claimed to be **Superman** after he died in the comics (Steel, The Man of Tomorrow, The Metropolis Kid and The Last Son of Krypton)

2814.1

Hal Jordan's official **Green Lantern** number

Three RottenTomatoes.com superhero film stinkers

GREEN LANTERN
(2011) **26% Fresh**

HOWARD THE DUCK
(1986) **14% Fresh**

BATMAN & ROBIN
(1997) **11% Fresh**

IF
PETER PARKER
WAS
15 IN 1962,
HE SHOULD NOW BE A GREY OLD MAN OF
69
YEARS OLD

THREE
WORDS SPOKEN BY
GROOT
IN *GUARDIANS OF THE GALAXY*
"I AM GROOT!"

48,502

Official estimated of enemies punished by
THE PUNISHER,
taken in 2011

40.761122, -73.982091
GOOGLE MAP CO-ORDINATES FOR MARVEL HQ

FOUR FANTASTIC BUDGETS

$1 MILLION
THE FANTASTIC FOUR
(1994)

$100 MILLION
FANTASTIC FOUR
(2005)

$130 MILLION
FANTASTIC FOUR:
RISE OF THE
SILVER SURFER (2007)

$122 MILLION
FANTASTIC FOUR
(2015)

Lynda Carter notched up approximately **2,907 minutes** of screen time in TV's *Wonder Woman*

That's **2,864** more than **Adrianne Palicki** spent as Wonder Woman in the never-broadcast 2011 TV pilot

OCTOBER 24 1929

BLADE'S BIRTHDAY!
Good luck blowing out them candles, *GRANDAD!*

DAREDEVIL #168
first appearance of Elektra

1988
Guardians' **Peter Quill** was abducted from Earth

50%
OF *JUDGE DREDD* FILMS IN WHICH WE SEE THE LAWMAN'S FACE

3,207,851, 900%
INCREASE IN VALUE:
A 10 CENT-BOUGHT
MINT COPY OF

Action Comics #1

WHICH SOLD ON *EBAY* FOR A WHOPPING

$3.2 million

US $130
Original amount paid to Siegel and Schuster for *Superman* rights by DC

3 MILLION
ESTIMATED DEATH TOLL OF NEW YORK IN WATCHMEN

JANUARY 1976

First **Marvel/DC** Superhero Team-Up: **Superman Vs The Amazing Spider-Man**

0 – TIMES

Cesar Romero shaved off his moustache to play **The Joker**

FOUNDING YEARS

1934 — DC (as National Allied Publications)

1939 — Marvel (as Timely Publications)

1986 — Dark Horse Comics

1992 — Image Comics

1999 — IDW Publishing

SEND A SUPERHERO A POSTCARD!

AVENGERS MANSION
980 Fifth Avenue, NY

STARK TOWER
58th and Broadway, nr Columbus Circle, NY

BAXTER BUILDING
42nd St and Madison Avenue, Manhattan

TWENTY-FIVE

To date, the number of times that comics icon **Stan Lee** has been seen in Marvel-related films and TV shows

FOUR AGES OF COMICS

GOLDEN AGE — 1938 - 1955
Heroes created: Superman, Batman, The Flash, Wonder Woman, Captain America

SILVER AGE — 1956 - 1969
Heroes created: Spider-Man, Incredible Hulk, Justice League of America, The X-Men, Fantastic Four, Daredevil

BRONZE AGE — 1970 - 1984
Heroes created: Luke Cage, The Punisher, Swamp Thing

DARK/MODERN AGE — 1985 - PRESENT
Heroes created: Deadpool, Hellboy, Hellblazer, Spawn

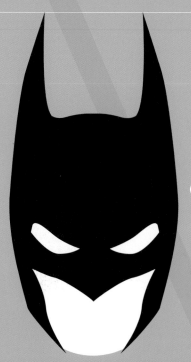

AGES OF BATMAN ACTOR AT START OF FILMING

ADAM WEST — **37**

MICHAEL KEATON — **37**

VAL KILMER — **34**

GEORGE CLOONEY — **35**

CHRISTIAN BALE — **30**

BEN AFFLECK — **41**

AVERAGE SCREEN BATMAN AGE: 36

ISSUE #27

DETECTIVE COMICS IN WHICH **BATMAN** DEBUTED

DEADPOOL ISSUE WHICH BOASTS A **GUINNESS WORLD RECORD**-BREAKING COUNT FOR NUMBER OF CHARACTERS FEATURED ON A COVER – A BANK BALANCE-CRIPPLING WEDDING GUEST LIST OF 232. (THE ISSUE CHEEKILY REFERS TO ITSELF AS, **"THE MOST IMPORTANT ISSUE #27 IN THE HISTORY OF COMICS!"**)

ORIGINAL LINE-UPS ASSEMBLE!

JUSTICE LEAGUE — 7
(Aquaman, Batman, Flash, Green Lantern, the Martian Manhunter, Superman and Wonder Woman)

AVENGERS — 5
(Iron Man, Hulk, Ant-Man, Wasp, Thor)

X-MEN — 5
(Cyclops, Jean Grey, Angel, Beast, Iceman. Professor X doesn't count, apparently)

INCREDIBLE HULK

DR BRUCE BANNER GROWS **26.5 INCHES** IN HEIGHT AND GAINS A WHOPPING **1272LBS** WHEN HE TRANSFORMS INTO THE...

6412

Lex Luthor's prisoner number in **Superman IV**: **The Quest For Peace**

Follow!

@TheRealStanLee
2.32 million followers

@Marvel
3.91 million followers

@DCComics
1.91 million followers

£75,000

Drop in value of a single tear in a copy of **Action Comics** #1

2000 AD

has had nine "**Thargs**" so far

10:3

The male to female ratio of characters in **Marvel** & **DC** comics

CAPTAIN AMERICA

The 'First Avenger' stands for truth, justice and freedom

First appeared: Captain America Comics #1
(published in March 1941 by Marvel Comics)

Originally named 'Super American', Cap was created by Joe Simon and Jack Kirby. Steve was created to battle the Nazis and spent most of the 1940s and 1950s doing just that. Realising that the character needed to move on, however, the writers moved him into the (then) modern world of the 1960s. Here he's something of a fish out of water, with his old time morality leading to him sometimes clashing with those around him. In the cataclysmic superhero civil war he chose to stand against the Superhero Registration Act (which saw heroes forced to reveal their secret identities) and came to blows with his friend Iron Man. With the war over he was shockingly killed by his friend Sharon Carter, who had been brainwashed by Doctor Faustus. However, it was later revealed that he was, in fact, not dead but phasing in and out of time and he soon returned to fight the good fight.

SECRET ORIGIN

Steve Rogers was a young man in the 1940s. Concerned by the rise of the Nazis, he enlisted in the US Army, where he was selected for "Project: Rebirth" - an experimental project trialling a new 'Super-Soldier serum'. It transformed Steve from a scrawny young man into a perfect specimen of a human: strong, smart and fit for any task. Years later, he ends up frozen in a block of ice, but was defrosted in the present day, his Super-Soldier powers having kept him alive for decades.

ALLIES

Bucky Barnes was Steve's childhood friend and sidekick, who was later brainwashed and turned into the deadly Winter Soldier. Sam Wilson (aka Falcon) is another heroic friend - and is the current Captain America in the comics. Sharon Carter (aka Agent 13) is the niece of Steve's old love, Peggy, and an ace SHIELD secret agent.

SKILLS AND POWERS

Cap's Super-Soldier serum gives him enhanced strength and agility. Added to that is his expert fighting and shooting skills, and his Vibranium-steel alloy shield makes for both excellent protection and a useful additional weapon.

ENEMIES

Cap spent many years battling the forces of HYDRA - the sinister, Nazi alternative to SHIELD - but while World War 2 may be over, their forces are still active in the Marvel world. His prime opponents the Red Skull (Johann Schmidt), Armin Zola and Baron Zemo all have ties to that organisation and continue to battle him to this day. Doctor Faustus, meanwhile, is a psychiatrist and criminal mastermind.

11

OF THE COOLEST MOMENTS IN...

CAPTAIN AMERICA: CIVIL WAR

Just eleven? For this movie, we could've chosen about fifty!

What happens when two of Earth's mightiest heroes face off? Sides are taken, with our favourite characters teaming up to fight their strongest foes yet – each other! Yes, Civil War is the best Marvel movie so far, and we've chosen our favourite eleven moments – and best hero – that took our breath away.

#1 BLACK WIDOW ESCAPES A TANK

Black Widow is trapped inside a tank with two goons and a live grenade that's about to blow! But Widow easily beats up the two goons and leaps to safety. We're starting to wonder if an explosion could even scratch her.

#2 "THIS IS YOUR PILOT SPEAKING, WE SEEM TO BE HAVING SOME TAKE OFF ISSUES"

At one point Bucky tries to escape via helicopter, so Captan America sprints up to it, leaps, grabs the helicopter and pulls it out of the sky! He struggles to cancel this flight at first, but ultimately even a helicopter is no match for the Captain.

#3 ANT-MAN MEETS CAPTAIN AMERICA

We like to imagine we'd act cool if we met Captain America. But honestly? We'd totally geek out and beg him for a selfie. That's what makes Ant-Man meeting Captain America so great – he geeks out too, crying "this is awesome!".

FACT!

AT JUST 19 YEARS OLD, TOM HOLLAND IS THE YOUNGEST EVER ACTOR TO PLAY SPIDER-MAN!

Bucky was the terrifying bad guy in The Winter Solider, a brainwashed assassin that even Black Widow couldn't stop. Though he's still not quite a hero, he heroically sacrifices his metal arm to save Captain America. Now that's brave! We wouldn't even sacrifice our fingernails.

HIMSELF

#5 "DID YOU EVER SEE THAT OLD MOVIE, THE EMPIRE STRIKES BACK?"

Spider-Man is a Star Wars fan! Of all the great lines webhead has in Civil War, this might be our favourite. It proves Peter Parker is a total nerd (nothing wrong with that) and gives him the idea for how to defeat Ant-Man. Speaking of which...

#6 ANT MAN TRIES A NEW SIZE

Instead of shrinking, as you'd expect from Ant-Man, he decides to bulk up, becoming a giant. He'd even make Hulk look puny! Spider-Man eventually trips him with webs, but until then, Ant-Man easily has this battle won for Team Cap.

#7 "WHO'S THE GUY IN THE CAT COSTUME?"

Yeah, there's no way you would say that to his face! Black Panther is brilliantly introduced. He's fast, has mad combat skills and his claws even manage to scratch Captain America's shield! Stay after the Civil War end credits for more Black Panther...

BEST HERO! SPIDER-MAN

With a new costume courtesy of Stark industries (good, Parker should be busy punching bad guys, not practising his needlework) Spidey is astonishing! One of the best fighters, and definitely the funniest, we can't wait for him to get his own movie.

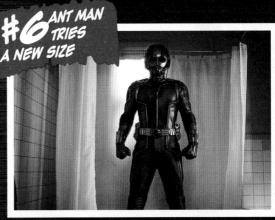

#9 "DON'T TELL AUNT MAY!"

Tony Stark invites himself over to Peter Parker's house for a little superhero man to man. Peter's fun, but we don't truly believe he's Spider-Man until he stops Tony leaving the room – by blasting him with webbing! Yep, that's definitely Spider-Man alright!

★
★
★
★
★
★
★
★

FACT!

WHEN IT'S AT FULL POWER, TONY STARK'S IRON MAN SUIT CAN LIFT OVER 100 TONS!

#8 SCARLET WITCH TAKES ON VISION

Vision is protecting Scarlet Witch from Hawkeye. Defeating the arrow-slinger is no problem, but what if Vision has to protect himself from Scarlet Witch? Now he's in trouble, as even he's no match for her mystical powers. Note to self: don't ever annoy witches (again)!

#10 MOTORWAY CHASE

Drive carefully, as Captain America, Black Panther and Falcon are on the road! Tracking down Bucky Barnes, the superheroes cause tons of car crash chaos in a spectacular chase. Hmm, actually, we think we'll get out and try walking today!

#11 THE BIG FIGHT

It's all come down to this, as Captain America and Iron Man go head to head. Armour is smashed and the hits hurt hard as these former friends become furious foes. Who wins? We'd have to be Loki levels of evil to spoil that...

MATCH THE SHADOWS!!!

The Avengers sure know how to strike an intimidating pose, even when shrouded in darkness, but who's shadow belongs to who? Match each hero with their shadowy counterpart to get them to assemble...

A **1** **2** **B**

C **3** **D** **4**

How to play

Match each lettered picture to its numbered shadow and then write your answer in the box. Have you managed to guess them all?

Write your answers here:

A .... **B** ....

C .... **D** ....

BOOM!

Answers: A=4 B=3 C=2 D=1

THOR

Everyone's favourite Asgardian god of thunder!

First appeared: Journey Into Mystery #83 (published August 1962 by Marvel Comics)

Inspired by Norse mythology, Stan Lee, Larry Lieber and Jack Kirby set out to create a new kind of superhero. The character they came up with was a clever mixture of old world magic and modern Marvel wit. Thor was always a popular character with fans, but he remained relatively obscure until the 2011 movie, starring Chris Hemsworth, brought him to the masses - now he's one of the biggest superheroes on the planet. The comics have continued to introduce new twists and turns and, in one surprising recent development, Thor has been found unworthy and been forced to hang up his hammer and change his name. He still does good, but he's now fighting evil as Odinson, while his sometime-girlfriend Jane Foster wields Mjolnir and the Thor name.

ALLIES

Thor has numerous friends and family in Asgard, including his father Odin, his wife Frigga and his half-brother Balder. He can also call on his colleagues in the Avengers and the members of the Warriors Three - Fandral, Hogun, and Volstagg, a team of three Asgardian adventurers. His romantic life is slightly complicated. The Asgardian warrior Sif often portrayed as his great love, but their relationship is strained because of his ties to Earth, and his feelings for Jane Foster, a human woman who falls for both Thor and Donald Blake (without realising that they are one and the same) and who now carries the name Thor.

SECRET ORIGIN

Thor is the Asgardian God Of Thunder. Arrogant and foolish, he was banished to Earth by his father Odin, where he merged with the human Donald Blake. With Thor's memories suppressed, Blake trained as a doctor until one day he found Thor's hammer, Mjolnir, and after smashing it against a rock transformed into Thor once more. Blake and Thor share their existence together, treating the sick and battling evil, although it was eventually revealed that Blake had really been an aspect of Thor all along.

SKILLS AND POWERS

Superhumanly strong and long-lived, Thor is also able to transport through dimensions, fly and change the weather. His hammer Mjolnir can only be wielded by someone who is truly worthy, and will always return to Thor when called.

ENEMIES

There's no Thor without Loki! The devious Asgardian trickster is Thor's adopted brother. Jealous, selfish and unpredictable, he's a truly challenging opponent who always has a trick up his sleeves. Malekith, the ruler of the Dark Elves has a bitter hatred of Odin and his family after his banishment to another dimension, and Mangog is an infinitely powerful being who was imprisoned beneath Asgard, but causes devastation whenever he is set free.

COOL STUFF!

You NEED this in your life!

Show off your love for the city's slickest web-slinger in this old-school Spiderman t-shirt,

Batman's always prepared – that's why this Batmobile can transform into the Batjet!

The Avengers Assemble Story Collection gives you the origins of your favourite heroes.

MEGA FAN!

This custom-made Iron Man Hulkbuster armour by Extreme Costumes is the *biggest* cosplay we've ever seen! It may not have actual rocket feet, but otherwise it's about as accurate as you can get.

WEIRD STUFF!

It's a little known fact, but cats love superheroes just as much as humans do - this one thought Civil War was so purr-fect that they let their owner dress them up as the Winter Soldier.

Bam! That's the sound of people's jaws hitting the floor when they see you with this backpack.

Practice your marksmanship with this less deadly version of Hawkeye's bow.

Recreate that epic fight in Lego with the Super Hero Airport Battle set.